Whole Language Series
People and Place

written by Linda Lee Maifair
illustrated by Priscilla Burris

LINDA LEE MAIFAIR received a Bachelor of Science degree and two Master of Arts degrees in reading and English from Indiana University of Pennsylvania. As a certified reading specialist, her background includes creative writing for young children and teens in children's magazines and writing for other educational publishers. As a freelance writer and consultant, she teaches creative writing classes at Wilson College in Chambersburg, Pennsylvania.

PRISCILLA BURRIS received an Associate of Arts degree in Creative Design from the Fashion Institute of Design and Merchandising in Los Angeles. As a free-lance artist of child-related artwork, she has been drawing since she was one year old. Priscilla lives in Southern California.

Copyright 1989 by **THE MONKEY SISTERS, INC.**
22971 Via Cruz
Laguna Niguel, CA 92677

ISBN 0-933606-72-9

The Writing Process

Pre-Writing: As a motivation to beginning any written work, use the introductory activity for each unit.

As a quick evaluation of the students' prior knowledge and as a teacher-guide for the gathering of resources and the selection of activities, brainstorm with your class using a question such as, "Tell me everything you know about. . . ." Record all responses and display the list.

Using the ideas gathered, collect as many resources as possible including fiction and non-fiction reading materials, realia, guest speakers, local exhibits or places to visit, etc. Based on these resources, students will begin the unit through teacher and student reading and sharing. The activities will foster the writing process.

Writing the Rough Draft: Writing suggestions to compliment the topic are included in each unit. Encourage writing through such questions as, "What do you already know?" and "What else do you want to know?"

Revising the Writing: Encourage partner-revising. Authors need audiences. The writer can read the rough draft and evaluate the listener's reactions through questions such as:

- What was my topic?
- Name three important things I wrote about my topic.
- What part was the most interesting?
- What part was confusing?
- What do you think I left out about my topic?

By receiving the listener's reactions, the writer can make decisions about what is strong in the written work and what information is weak, or perhaps, missing. Students should vary their audiences and the opportunities for revision help . . . classmates, teachers, students from other classes, parents, aides, etc.

Editing for Mechanics: Some natural editing is accomplished through the process of the student reading aloud during the revision stage. One of the most effective methods of editing one's own work is to simply read aloud to oneself.

Students with strengths in specific mechanical skills (capitalization, punctuation, spelling) can offer help to one another. The teacher should be considered the 'final editor!'

The Final Work: Ideas for final drafts are included with each unit. These can be shared in a variety of ways—library displays, sharing with another class, bulletin board displays, class booklets distributed to student's homes, etc. It is fun to include a sheet of paper encouraging comments from the reader to the writer.

People and Places

Introduction

The **Whole Language Series** consists of the following three titles and units:

Everyday Things	Living Things	People and Places
Wheels	Cattle	Helen Keller
Water	Spiders	Walt Disney
Windows	Penguins	Hans Christian Andersen
Paper	Dolphins	The Rocky Mountains
Popcorn	Wildflowers	New York City
Parties	Trees	The Great Lakes

Each of the six units contains an outline/guide sheet which gives an introduction and overview of the unit. For each page of activity, the guide sheet lists the curriculum area/skill, type of activity and page number. A suggested culminating activity is given.

As each unit's contents are varied, different curriculum areas will be focused upon based on the topic. In each one, however, a variety of subject is covered. We encourage these ideas to be expanded upon or eliminated based on the grade level and ability of your class.

Due to the variety of material presented, we suggest the following be considered with these grade levels:

Grades 2-3: Activities may be more large group/class oriented.

Grades 3-4: Activities may be more small group/individually oriented.

Grades 4-5: Activities are more individually oriented. Some lessons will still lend themselves to class projects.

Round out these teaching units by setting up a center in your classroom with library books, photographs, charts, samples and other items of interest to provide motivation to the unit. Show filmstrips, videos or films of the topic being studied and explore other centers of interest outside the classroom to enhance the study further.

TABLE OF CONTENTS

HELEN KELLER

INTRODUCTION: As a group, list the things a person would be unable to do if he or she was blind or deaf. If possible, view *The Miracle Worker,* and cross off those things Helen Keller learned to do. Discuss how she lost her sight and hearing, why her teacher was considered a miracle worker, and the difference in her life and personality after she learned to use language.

CULMINATION: Have students use what they know about Helen Keller to refute some common myths about handicapped people:
   • People with handicaps should be treated differently.
   • People with handicaps aren't as smart as other people.
   • People with handicaps can't do things 'normal' people can do.
   • People with handicaps don't enjoy things other people do.
   • People with handicaps have dull and useless lives.

Read aloud from Helen Keller's essay, "Three Days to See."

WHAT I'D MISS MOST

Helen Keller was born with normal sight and hearing. At a young age, a high fever left her blind and deaf. Think about the things you would miss seeing, hearing and doing if you suddenly could not see or hear.

On the lines below, write a paragraph of 6-8 sentences about the things you would miss *most* if you were blind and deaf.

What I'd Miss Most

There are many things I would miss if I couldn't see

or hear. _____

_____

_____

_____

_____

_____

_____

_____

_____

_____

_____

_____

SEEING FINGERS
A Lesson in Learning and Touching

1. Discuss how Helen Keller used her fingers to "see."

2. Read the classic poem, *The Blind Men and the Elephant.* Discuss why each man got such a different 'picture' of the elephant. Have students suppose the blind men had seen a pony or cow. What would the men have compared the animal to if they had each 'examined' different parts of these animals?

3. Blindfold three students. Give them an assortment of fabric and paper swatches— one at a time. (tissue paper, waxed paper, plastic wrap, aluminum foil, corduroy, silk, sandpaper, terry cloth, etc.) After each student has had a chance to 'look at' each sample, have them guess what the material is and explain how they could tell without seeing it.

4. Change students. Pass out a number of common objects. Have students guess what the objects are and explain how they knew. (book, telephone, toy car, balloon, pencil, hat, cup, banana, comb, shower cap, sock, straw, rubber bank, crayon, etc.) Change students; make some objects easily identifiable, others more difficult.

5. Select one student. Give him or her two similar objects . . . book/magazine, soccer ball/volley ball, apple/orange, nail/screw, silk flower/real flower, etc. Have student tell how they are alike and different. Change student for each pair of objects.

6. Choose three new students. Give each an assortment of four or five different-sized blocks. Have them arrange the blocks in order—smallest to largest. Still blindfolded, have them try to stack the blocks, largest to smallest.

7. Give each of several students a different model animal. Have each one guess what animal is being held and explain the basis for the guess before removing the blindfold.

8. Give each of several students a different toy vehicle. Have students guess the vehicle and justify his/her guess.

9. Blindfold a subject. Choose a classmate. Have the subject 'look at' the classmate's face as Helen Keller did—with her hands—and guess who the classmate is.

10. Have all students bring in a large handkerchief or scarf to use as a blindfold. Have each student, blindfolded, sculpt a common object or animal from a piece of clay. Then have students guess what each other's sculpture is supposed to be prior to displaying them. Identify each sculture with a tag when projects are completed.

LET YOUR FINGERS DO THE TALKING

Helen Keller not only had to learn a special written alphabet called *Braille*, she had to learn to 'read' finger spelling with her hands instead of her eyes. In school, she 'heard' her lessons by having her teacher, Annie Sullivan, spell out each word of the lecture, one letter at a time, and she wrote out her answers without being able to see them.

To get an idea of how long and hard Helen's lessons were, do the following: (1) Pick a long paragraph from your science or social studies book. Have someone spell it out to you by 'writing' the letters on your palm with their fingertip. (2) Write your name and address with your eyes closed.

The sign language below has been developed to help deaf people communicate. Try to form each letter. Then try to spell out your name and finally spell out a question to a classmate.

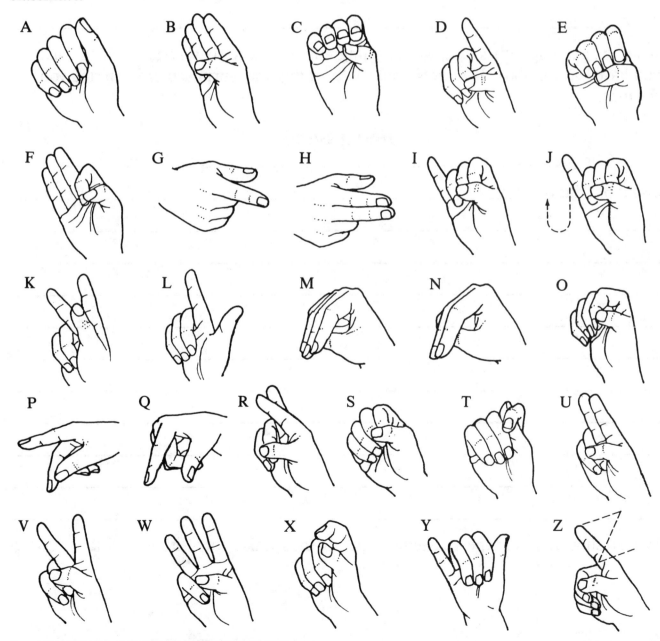

BE OUR GUEST

Even though Helen Keller could not hear, she learned to speak. In fact, she gave lectures to audiences all over the world. If Helen Keller had visited this class, what would you have asked her?

1. _____

2. _____

A visitor has been invited to talk to the class about blindness. Think about what you would like to know about being blind, modern schools for blind people, reading Braille, using a guide dog, or doing everyday things like dressing, cooking, shopping, working, etc. What two questions would you like the guest speaker to answer?

1. _____

2. _____

After the guest speaker's visit, write a paragraph of four to six sentences telling what you have learned about blindness. Include the things that surprised or interested you the most.

Being Blind

    Our guest speaker, _____, told us many things about blindness. _____

_____

_____

_____

_____

_____

_____

_____

_____

_____

Write a short note, or tape a cassette, thanking the speaker for visiting.

Name _____

OUR FIVE SENSES WORTH

Humans have five ways of experiencing things. These are called our five senses. Which two senses did Helen Keller lose?

_____ and _____

What three senses did she rely on to learn about her world?

_____, _____, and _____

Suppose you were experiencing orange juice for the first time. What would each of your senses tell you about orange juice?

A. Sight: _____   B. Hearing: _____

C. Touch: _____   D. Smell: _____

          E. Taste: _____

If you were to outline what you know about the sense of sight, it might look like the outline below on the left. See if you can fill in the blank outlines for the other four senses.

Sight

I. Organ—the eyes

II. Information—colors, sizes, shapes

III. Uses—reading, writing, drawing, driving, sports

IV. Loss—blindness

Hearing

I. _____

II. _____

III. _____

IV. _____

Touch

I. _____

II. _____

III. _____

IV. _____

Smell

I. _____

II. _____

III. _____

IV. _____

Taste

I. _____

II. _____

III. _____

IV. _____

DOGGONE GOOD EYES AND EARS

Helen Keller had a human companion. She not only 'translated' what people said into finger spelling to help Helen communicate, but also acted as a guide. Today many blind people have specially-trained dogs to guide them safely from place to place, and many deaf people have dogs to alert them to sounds and dangers they cannot hear. From what you have read or seen—and by thinking about the things a person has to do each day— see if you can list three ways each type of guide dog can help his owner. What ways can the dog make his owner's life easier or safer?

Seeing Eye Dog	**Hearing Dog**
1. _____	1. _____
2. _____	2. _____
3. _____	3. _____

Add three to four sentences to each paragraph below to explain how guide dogs for the blind and deaf are alike or different.

Dogs for Eyes and Ears

Guide dogs for the deaf and blind are alike in many ways.

_____
_____
_____
_____
_____
_____
_____
_____

Guide dogs for the deaf and blind are different in many ways.

_____
_____
_____
_____
_____
_____
_____
_____

What qualities do you think a good guide dog should have?

People and Places © THE MONKEY SISTERS, INC.

WOMEN OF COURAGE

Kitty O'Neill lost her hearing after getting measles, mumps and smallpox when she was a baby. Although she couldn't hear, she learned to talk. Kitty didn't think her deafness should stop her from doing what other people do. By the time she was in third grade, she was going to a regular school. She learned to play the cello and piano by feeling the vibrations and became such a good diver she came in eighth in the 1964 Olympics. When she got spinal meningitis, doctors thought she would never walk again, but she did. Kitty had to give up diving, she she didn't give up sports. In 1970, she set the women's speed skiing record going 104 miles per hour. In 1976, she set the women's land speed record, hitting a speed of 618 miles per hour. As a Hollywood stuntwoman, Kitty performed stunts for both TV series, Wonder Woman and The Bionic Woman. In fact, for a Wonder Woman stunt, she did a free fall 127 feet onto an airbag—the only woman to try the stunt from such a height. Kitty once said that deafness wasn't a handicap, it was a challenge.

What five words would you use to describe Kitty O'Neill?

_____, _____, _____, _____, and _____.

What five words would you use to describe Helen Keller?

_____, _____, _____, _____, and _____.

Write a paragraph explaining at least three things that Helen Keller and Kitty O'Neill have in common.

Two Women of Courage

Helen Keller and Kitty O'Neill have many things in common. _____

_____

_____

_____

_____

_____

_____

_____

_____

_____

_____

DRUGS FOR BUGS

When Helen Keller was a child, there were no *antibiotics* or even common medicines like aspirin. There was little doctors could do to stop the fever that destroyed her sight and hearing. Today, we have many 'miracle drugs' that can prevent and cure serious illnesses such as the fever that Helen Keller had. Let's look at what a mother would do if her child had a fever today:

She would need to find out if the child really has a fever. The normal temperature for a person is 98.6°F. Read the thermometers below to see what each child's temperature is. Put a check in the box next to those who have a fever, a temperature over 98.6.

☐ Billy's temperature   98.6°   ☐ Sally's temperature   101°

☐ Sherry's temperature   98°   ☐ Mike's temperature   102°

Mom would have to figure out how much medicine Sally and Mike need to take. She would do that by reading the chart on the right.

Age	2-3	4-5	6-8	9-10	11-12
Wt. Lbs.	24-35	36-47	48-59	60-71	72-95
Tablets	2	3	4	5	6

Sally is 8 years old. Mom would give her _____ tablets.

Mike weighs 42 pounds. Mom would give him _____ tablets.

How old are you? _____ How much do you weigh? _____

How many tablets would you need?

What might happen if you took too few? _____

What might happen if you took too many? _____

The tablets can be taken every four hours. If Mom gave Mike and Sally their medicine at 9 am, when would they take it again?

_____ o'clock, then _____ o'clock, then _____ o'clock

The chart says you can take the tablets five times a day. How many tablets would Sally take in a day? _____ Mike? _____

I Think I Can, I Think I Can

What did *The Little Engine* do that nobody thought he could do?

_____

_____

What did Helen Keller do that nobody thought she could do?

_____

_____

What are two things that you have learned to do that, at first, you never thought you could do? (Or two things that somebody else said you couldn't do, and you proved you could!)

1. _____   2. _____

Write a paragraph about something you would like to do in the future. This can be something new you would like to learn now (swimming, playing the guitar), something you would like to accomplish (be an Eagle Scout), or something you would like to do as an adult (be a doctor or an astronaut). Tell why you want to do this thing, some of the challenges you will face, how you will feel when you reach your goal, or what makes you think you can do it.

I Think I Can!

If I try hard enough, I think I can _____

_____

_____

_____

_____

_____

_____

_____

_____

_____

Walt Disney

INTRODUCTION: Have a variety of Disney storybooks available for students to read during the unit. Students may bring in books to share from their home libraries. View an old Mickey Mouse Club segment or a Wonderful World of Disney film in which Walt Disney introduced the show or explained some aspect of the animation or characters.

CULMINATION: Have a 'Disney Day'. Students can: (1) dress as their favorite Disney character and have a parade for the school; (2) have a Disney film festival showing both a cartoon and a non-animated adventure or comedy (*Shaggy Dog, Absent Minded Professor.*) Older students could read the book first (*Treasure Island, Swiss Family Robinson, Johnny Tremain, etc.*) and compare with the film. You may also: (3) hold a Disney songfest playing recordings and/or singing theme songs to Disney films and TV shows; (4) plan and carry out a "Wish Upon a Star" class project making a wish come true for someone (residents of a local nursing home, a sick child, etc.).

Wish Upon a Star

Walt Disney didn't let anything keep him from his dreams of owning a movie studio, producing good movies for children, and building a new kind of amusement park for families to enjoy together. Many Disney films have magical creatures who make wishes come true. Can you name some of these stories? Even his theme song, *"When You Wish Upon a Star,"* has to do with dreams coming true, for everybody.

> *When you wish upon a star*
> *Makes no difference who you are*
> *When you wish upon a star*
> *Your dreams come true.*

Below is a wishing star. Each point of the star has a different dream to wish for. Finish each wish with your own special dreams. Draw a picture of yourself or paste a photo of yourself in the center. Wish upon your star, and maybe your dreams will come true!

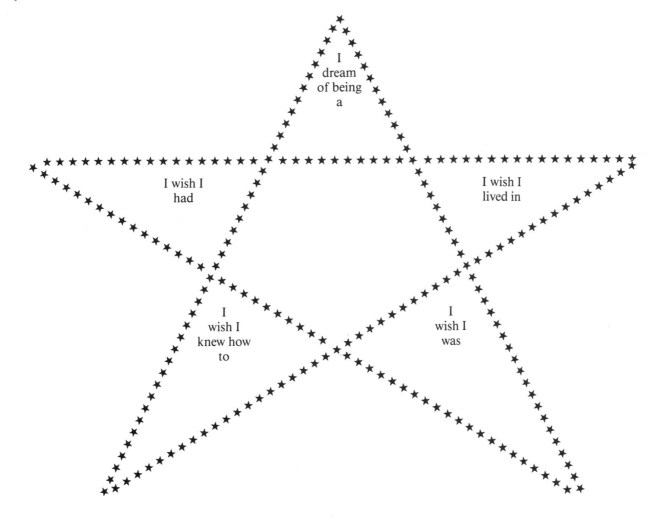

Name _____

Once Upon a Time

If you wrote a *summary* of your favorite Disney animated film, you would try to tell the whole story in a few sentences. You would tell the most important events in the order they happened. For example:

Snow White: A jealous queen tells her huntsman to kill Snow White, but he leaves her in the woods instead. She finds the cabin of the Seven Dwarfs and becomes their friend. When the wicked queen finds out Snow White is still alive, she disguises herself as an old woman and gives her a poison apple. Snow White falls into a deep sleep. The Seven Dwarfs are very sad until a handsome prince awakens Snow White with a kiss and marries her.

Choose one of these Disney stories: Cinderella, Bambi, The Fox and The Hound, 101 Dalmations, The Lady and the Tramp, Pinocchio or Sleeping Beauty. Tell the whole story in 100 words or less. Illustrate the border with scenes from the story.

(Title) _____

_____

_____

_____

_____

_____

_____

_____

_____

_____

_____

_____

_____

_____

_____

_____

Happy Birthday

In the Disney movie, *Peter Pan,* Peter never wanted to grow up. As a cartoon character, he never will! He will always stay the way he was when the movie first came out in 1953. But, Peter *is* older. Just how old is he? To find out anyone's age, all you have to do is subtract the year he or she was born from the current year.

For example, *Peter Pan* came out in 1953. If this is 1989, you would subtract:

  1989 current year
 − 1953 birth year
  36 years old in 1989

The first Mickey Mouse cartoon was in 1928. How old would Mickey be in 1989?

  1989 current year
 − 1928 birth year
  61 years old in 1989

Other Disney cartoon movie characters are a lot older than they look, too. How old are these favorites:

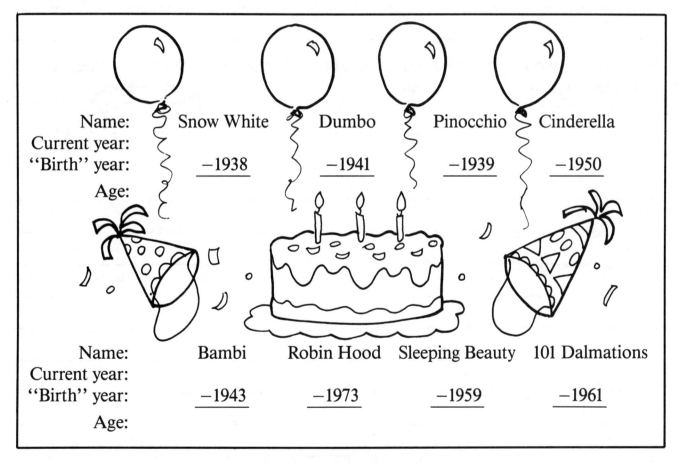

	Snow White	Dumbo	Pinocchio	Cinderella
Name:				
Current year:				
"Birth" year:	−1938	−1941	−1939	−1950
Age:				

	Bambi	Robin Hood	Sleeping Beauty	101 Dalmations
Name:				
Current year:				
"Birth" year:	−1943	−1973	−1959	−1961
Age:				

HOW OLD ARE *YOU*?

What year were you born? (Subtract your age from this year) _____

What year will you be able to drive? _____ to vote? _____

The Legend of Davy Crockett

A favorite Disney film and television character, Davy Crockett, was a real-life frontiersman, politician, and hero. Although Crockett really lived, like most legends (stories of real or imaginary heroes, passed down from one generation to the next), his feats were greatly exaggerated. Can you find the truth behind "The Legend of Davy Crockett?"

Things that are exaggerated in "The Legend of Davy Crockett."

1. _____

_____

2. _____

_____

3. _____

_____

Things that really happened in "The Legend of Davy Crockett."

1. _____

_____

2. _____

_____

3. _____

_____

Write a paragraph of four to six sentences about the real Davy Crockett—things you found out in your reading or research.

The Real Davy Crockett

_____

_____

_____

_____

_____

_____

_____

_____

_____

_____

_____

Flip Your Lid!

An animated cartoon is really a series of pictures—more than 360 separate illustrations for each minute of cartoon. You can make your own animated cartoon of a man taking off his hat and putting it on again.

1. Finish blocks 3, 4 and 5 so that the hat moves a little in each block, until it is all the way off in block 6.
2. In blocks 7, 8, 9 and 10, move the hat a little toward the man's head until he has it on again.
3. Cut the page into 12 blocks and paste onto index cards or heavy paper that can bend easily.
4. Put the blocks in order. Staple on the top or left side.
5. Flip the pages to see your 'animated cartoon.'

Toy Shop

Walt Disney's father did not believe in toys or entertainment. He made his children work hard for their food and clothes and took a strap to them when they disobeyed or 'wasted' their time playing. Since he had no toys, Walt made believe the animals on his farm could talk to him, just like Mickey Mouse or Donald Duck. When he was delivering newspapers early each morning, he played with the toys other children left out in their yards. But his favorite toy was his imagination. When Walt Disney grew up, he used his imagination to entertain children, and one of his most popular films, *Pinocchio*, is about a toy that comes to life.

Suppose you had no toys and had to make your own from odds and ends you found around the house. Use your imagination—and as many of the following items as you want, but nothing else!—to make a toy. What will you make? A robot? A rocket ship? A vehicle? A doll or puppet? A play house?

empty boxes	empty cans	milk containers
glue	tape	construction paper
cardboard	yarn/string	old socks (clean ones!)
straws	paper cups	ice cream sticks
crayons	paint	markers
tin foil	cloth scraps	empty thread spools
cotton balls	buttons	pillow stuffing
jar lids	scissors	margarine bowls

After your toy is finished, give it a name. Then list the steps (in order) in making the toy so that someone else could make one for himself by following your directions.

How to Make a _____

1. _____
2. _____
3. _____
4. _____
5. _____
6. _____
7. _____
8. _____

Crazy Ideas

People thought Walt Disney was crazy for making the film, *Snow White,* the first full-length cartoon movie, but Walt Disney believed in new ideas. In fact, at Disney World and Disneyland, Tommorowland features new ideas of the future—today's crazy ideas that might be tomorrow's greatest inventions and achievements.

Here are some other inventors who were thought to be crazy because they had new, untried ideas. Research each one. See what his 'crazy' idea was and why it turned out to be a good idea after all.

Name	'Crazy' Ideas	Why Important
Alexander Graham Bell		
Robert Fulton		
Benjamin Franklin		
Wright Brothers		
Thomas Edison		
Henry Ford		

Some Not-So-Crazy Ideas

List what you think are the three most important inventions in the modern world. Then look up each invention and see if you can find out whose 'crazy idea' it was.

Crazy Idea	Inventor
1. _____	_____
2. _____	_____
3. _____	_____

Making Movies

Walt Disney was an animator and producer of his films. He performed on the "Wonderful World of Disney" show. He was even the voice of Mickey Mouse. Listed below are some careers in the motion picture industry. Describe the work each person plays in making films.

Scriptwriter: _____

Actor/Actress: _____

Director: _____

Animator: _____

Costume Designer: _____

Make-up Artist: _____

Choreographer: _____

Cameraman: _____

Stuntman/Stuntwoman: _____

Write a paragraph telling which of these film careers you would choose. Tell why you would like that job or why it suits you best.

My Role in the Movies

If I could have a job in the movies, I would want to be a _____

_____

_____

_____

_____

_____

_____

_____

_____

People and Places © THE MONKEY SISTERS, INC.

Whistle While You Work

Heigh Ho! Heigh Ho! It's off to work you go! Suppose, like Walt Disney's father, your parents decided you had to go out and work for your food, clothes and even the roof over your head! (Walt wasn't allowed to keep any of the money he made, either.) The first thing you might do is look in the 'want ads' section of the local newspaper to see if there was a job you could do. When you found one, you would write a letter of application telling the person who placed the ad why you would like the job and why you should get it.

1. Look at these 'want ad' titles. Find a job you might apply for.
2. Write a letter telling what qualifications or experience you have and why you would like the job.

HELP WANTED

Dishwasher	Babysitter	Snow Shoveler	Grass Cutter	Clown
Delivery Person	Laundry Assistant	Newspaper Carrier		Model
Dog Walker	Baker's Helper	Car Washer	Singer	Actor

Dear Sir:

    I would like to apply for the position of _____

    I think I would be good at this job because _____

_____

_____

_____

    I would like to have this job because _____

_____

_____

_____

_____

                              Sincerely,

_____

Hans Christian Andersen

INTRODUCTION: If possible, view the Walt Disney movie, *Hans Christian Andersen* starring Danny Kaye. Read aloud three or four of Hans Christian Andersen's tales.

CURRICULUM AREA/SKILLS:	ACTIVITY/TITLE	PAGE NO.

Bulletin board "No Ugly Ducklings" 22

Students tape a photo of themselves as an infant on the small duck outline. On the large swan outline, students finish "The Beauty Inside Me" (their good qualities) and "The Swan I'll Someday Be" (their dreams of the future). Display on bulletin board without names so students can guess who the "ducklings are."

Language Arts "Twisted Tales" 23

Students list six important events from their favorites Andersen tale out of sequence. Exchanging lists with a classmate, they try to put the twisted tales back into sequential order.

Language arts; biography "Author, Author" 24

Based on the Danny Kaye movie, biographical material provided by the teacher, or information found in reference books, students fill out biographical sketches of Hans Christian Andersen, then research a second author of their choice. (You may want to provide a suggested list of authors).

Math "How Much Would You Need?" 25

Students list the expenses they would have and add up how much it would cost if they lived on their own.

Social studies; geography "Here and There" 26

Students research and compare Denmark with their own country. You may wish to lead in with a film about Denmark.

Science; language arts "Not Quite" 27

Students compare creatures, like the duck and the swan, which are similar but not quite the same. Creative writing story ideas are included as a follow-up activity.

Language arts; poetry "Rhyme Time" 28

Students complete two-line rhymes about mermaids and other mythical creatures.

Language arts; outlining "Create-A-Creature" 29

Students create a mythical creature of their own describing the creature in outline form, then illustrate it.

Language arts "Puppet Plays" 30

This teacher resource sheet explains a group activity writing script versions of Andersen tales, creating stick-puppet characters, and acting them out for the rest of the class.

CULMINATION: Take the puppet plays 'on the road' performing them for students in younger classes, the school parent organization, a local nursing home or children's hospital, etc. You may also wish to have students read other popular fairy tales (The Brothers Grimm, etc.) or popular folk tales from their own cultural, ethnic backgrounds.

No Ugly Ducklings

The Ugly Duckling was treated badly because he was different. No one could see the beautiful swan he would become or the beautiful creature he was inside.

Hans Christian Andersen was a very poor and homely boy. People often made fun of the way he looked or the old clothes he had to wear. They couldn't see the beautiful person Andersen was inside. But Andersen didn't give up. He believed in himself and his dream of being a writer. He knew he would become a beautiful *swan* some day.

Each of us is beautiful in some way. Each of us has a dream. Inside the swan outline below, describe the beauty inside you (talents, good points) and the dream you have for your future:

-- Cut Here --

The beauty

inside me is

that I'm _____

_____

_____

_____

_____

_____

The swan I'll someday be is _____

_____

_____

_____

_____

Tape a picture of you when you were just a "duckling."

Twisted Tales

A storyteller must tell his story in order . . . the first thing that happened, then the next, and so on until he gets to the end. The story would make no sense if he told what happened last, first, and what happened first, last.

How good a storyteller are you? Read a tale by Hans Christian Andersen. Then, on the left, list six important things that happened in your favorite Andersen story. Read through the list and make sure you have the events in order. Now, see how well a classmate can put things in order. On the right, list the same six events from the story but mix them up this time. (The more you jumble the order, the better.) Fold the page in half so your friend can't peek at the answers and exchange papers. Try to put each other's stories in order again, by numbering the events correctly from one to six.

Title: _____

1. _____
   _____
2. _____
   _____
3. _____
   _____
4. _____
   _____
5. _____
   _____
6. _____
   _____

Title: _____

1. _____
   _____
2. _____
   _____
3. _____
   _____
4. _____
   _____
5. _____
   _____
6. _____
   _____

Fold Back Here

Author! Author!

A biography tells the story of someone's life. See if you can fill in the biography of Hans Christian Andersen on the left. Then look up another author of children's stories (your teacher or school librarian can give you some suggestions) and complete the biography on the right.

HANS CHRISTIAN ANDERSEN

was born in _____

in the year _____ .

    His family was _____

and _____ . As a child

he was very _____ and

_____ .

    Two problems he had to overcome

were _____

and _____

_____ .

    He is best known for stories

that are _____ .

The titles of two of his stories

are _____

_____ and _____

_____ .

    The most interesting thing

I learned about Hans Christian

was _____

_____

_____ .

_____

was born in _____

in the year _____ .

    His/her family was _____

and _____ . As a child

he/she was very _____ and

_____ .

    Two problems he/she had to over-

come were _____

_____ and _____

_____ .

    He/She is known for stories that

are _____ .

The titles of two of his/her stories

are _____

_____ and _____

_____ .

    The most interesting thing I

learned about _____

was _____

_____

_____ .

How Much Would You Need?

Hans Christian Andersen was given a government 'allowance' so he could work on his writing. He lived very simply and didn't need much money for his food, clothes, rent, and other expenses.

How much allowance or *salary* (pay for a job) would you need to live on your own? On the left below, list some of the things you would need—some of the *expenses* you would have.

Expense	**Cost** (for a month)
1. Rent, a place to stay	1. $ _____
2. _____	2. $ _____
3. _____	3. $ _____
4. _____	4. $ _____
5. _____	5. $ _____
6. _____	6. $ _____

A. Look in the classified ads of your local newspaper to see how much it would cost to rent a room or small apartment for a month. Put the amount of your rent expense under *cost* on line 1 above.

B. Did you remember to put food on your list of expenses? Make up a shopping list for your food for a month. Then look at the grocery store ads in the paper or visit the grocery store to see how much your food would cost you. Or figure out what it would cost to eat at your favorite restaurant once a week or so. Put this amount next to your food expense.

C. *Estimate* (make a rough guess) how much the other expenses on your list would cost. Write down the amounts.

D. Add up your expenses to see the *minimum* (least or smallest) amount you would need each month.

People and Places © THE MONKEY SISTERS, INC.

Here and There

Hans Christian Andersen lived in Denmark. Is modern Denmark like your country or very different? Use the chart below to compare *here* (your country) with *there* (Denmark).

	Here	There
A. Size (square miles)		
B. Population		
C. Type of government		
D. Leader of government		
E. Capital		
F. Major cities (three)		
G. Divisions (states, provinces) How many?		
H. Language		
I. Industries, products		
J. Crops or livestock		
K. Sports/activities		
L. Special foods		
M. Famous sights, landmarks		
N. Famous events, people in history		
O. Picture of country's flag		

Not Quite

In Hans Christian Andersen's, *The Ugly Duckling*, the duckling wasn't a duckling at all. He was really a swan.

What do ducks and swans have in common? How are they alike?

A. _____   B. _____

C. _____   D. _____

How are ducks and swans different?

A. _____   B. _____

Here are some pairs of creatures that are very similar, but *not quite* the same. See if you can find out how they are different.

1. A dog and a wolf _____

_____

2. A horse and a donkey _____

_____

3. A butterfly and a moth _____

_____

4. A whale and a fish_____

_____

5. A toad and a frog _____

_____

Bonus: Write your own 'Ugly Duckling' story. Suppose your brother brought home a puppy that turned out to be a wolf, or a kitten that turned out to be a tiger. Suppose you were a donkey in a barn full of horses, or a toad in a pond full of frogs. Write a story about an ugly duckling who turned out different than everybody expected, or who wasn't quite the same as everyone else.

People and Places © THE MONKEY SISTERS, INC.

Rhyme Time

One of Hans Christian Andersen's most famous tales is about a mermaid. A mermaid is a *mythical* (made-up or legendary) creature who is part woman, part fish.

Below are the first lines of some rhymes about mermaids and other mythical creatures who appear in fairy tales and legends. See if you can write the second line to form a *couplet* (two-line poem). Here's a mermaid couplet as an example:

I caught a mermaid in a net
Her hair was long, and blonde and wet.

(or) *She was a sight I won't forget.*
(or) *Was I amazed? Surprised? You bet!*
(or) *How much luckier could I get?*
(or) *She asked me, "Is it lunchtime yet?"*

Now, you try it!

1. *A **mermaid** sat upon a rock*

   _____

2. *A **centaur** is part man, part horse*

   _____

3. *A **pegasus** knows how to fly*

   _____

4. *I wish I had a **unicorn***

   _____

5. *I met a **leprechaun** dressed in green*

   _____

6. *"Make three wishes," the **genie** said*

   _____

7. *The **dragon** snorted smoke and flame*

   _____

Try writing your own rhyme about one (or more) of these creatures: elf, sea serpent, witch, giant, bigfoot, gnome, fairy.

Create-A-Creature

Some fairy tale and mythical creatures are two creatures combined, like a mermaid or centaur. Some have magical powers, like genies, fairies and leprechauns. Some are exaggerations of real creatures, like giants or sea serpents.

Use your imagination to create your own creature. Fill out the outline below to describe the creature's looks, powers, habits, and personality. Then draw a picture of your creature. Be sure to give him/her a name that fits the sort of creature it is.

My _____
(creature's name)

My _____
(creature's name)

  I. Appearance

    A. _____

    B. _____

  II. Magical powers

    A. _____

    B. _____

  III. Where he/she lives

    A. _____

    B. _____

  IV. Unusual habits

    A. _____

    B. _____

  V. Personality (friendly, kind, greedy, shy, etc.)

    A. _____

    B. _____

Draw your creature here ↑

Puppet Plays

Although Hans Christian Andersen is best known for his fairy tales and children's stories, he was also a playwright, writing plays for adults. When he was young, he even dreamed of being an actor and acting out his own stories on the stage.

1. Divide the class into small groups.

2. Ask the class for titles of favorite Andersen tales. Write these on slips of paper. Have one member of each group draw a slip of paper to see which play the group will do, so each group will be working on a different play.

3. Each group should then:
   - list characters in the story, all the parts they'll need, (speaking and non-speaking), human and animal.
   - list the events of the story in order—everything they want to have happen in their play version.
   - write a script with those characters and a narrator, following their list of events with copies for each member of the group.
   - make stick puppets of each character
     —draw each character on tagboard or cardboard
     —cut out each character puppet
     —tape each puppet to a ruler, piece of dowel rod, or similar 'stick' handle.
   - Make stand-up, cardboard scenery (optional)
   - assign parts (everyone in group should get to read a part, work a puppet, or both.
   - rehearse the play—each group in a different area to keep the play 'secret' until Opening Night.

4. Drape a blanket or sheet over a large table or desk so that student puppeteers behind the table will not be visible. This is the 'stage.'

5. Each group performs its play for the rest of the class.

6. You may wish to have your own 'Tony Awards,' having each student vote on his/her favorite play (perhaps stipulating that students may not vote for their own play.)

Note: Plays may also be written and performed in 'costume'—the children acting out the parts themselves rather than making the stick puppets.

The Rocky Mountains

INTRODUCTION: View a travel or Park Service film on one of the national parks or view a film about the Rockies and famous landmarks in the area or a historical film such as the Lewis and Clark expedition. Discuss what students would expect to find in the mountains . . . what kind of animals would live there, what kind of crops would grow there, etc. Locate The Rocky Mountains on a map of North America or on a globe. Discuss concepts of *The Great Divide* (rivers on one side flow one way, on the other side they flow the opposite direction), *elevation* (compare the elevation of where they live to the highest peak in the Rockies), and *timberline* (the elevation beyond which trees will no longer grow.).

CURRICULUM AREA/SKILLS:	ACTIVITY/TITLE	PAGE NO.
Note taking; outlining	"What's in a Mountain?"	32

Students fill in a mountain outline with names of various places and things found in the Rockies. Color and display.

Social studies; map reading	"It's a Rocky World"	33

Students list states and provinces in the Rocky Mountain range and locate other major world mountain ranges and record elevation, length, location, etc.

Science; creative writing	"A Beastly Life"	34

Students research one Rocky Mountain animal and write a paragraph telling what their life would be like if they were that animal.

Cooking; research	"Rocky Mountain Recipes"	35

Students research a Rocky Mountain food product, then find and copy a recipe using that product. Students may wish to print and distribute a cookbook of these recipes or you may want to bring in ingredients such as raw beets, chili peppers and pinto beans for students to sample some of the recipes.

Social studies; research	"Rocky Resources"	36

Students look up uses for several Rocky Mountain natural resources and list names, locations and uses of natural resources in their own state or province.

Math; addition	"Eureka!"	37

Students imagine what it was like to be a gold prospector and add up the weights on several sets of scales to see how much gold they found. This could lead into a lesson using and reading various kinds of scales, adding weights, weight equivalents, etc.

Sports; writing	"Rocky Recreation"	38

Students choose one of several Rocky Mountain recreations, draw themselves engaged in a sport and answer questions about the sport they have chosen.

Arts and crafts	"Easy Indian Crafts"	39

Students make headbands, warrior medals and beads and read about one of the Indian tribes from the Rocky Mountains. Children may study Indian picture-writing and use what they learn to decorate their crafts.

Social studies; creative writing	"Westward Ho!"	40

Students answer questions about pioneer travel over the mountains and write a page in their journal as young pioneers making such a trip.

CULMINATION: Divide students into three or four groups to research and present oral reports on the following topics: Sacajawea, the Indian woman guide who led Lewis and Clark across the Rockies; other mountain ranges in North America; or a mountain myth such as Bigfoot or Paul Bunyan.

What's in a Mountain?

As you learn about the Rocky Mountains, fill in each section of the 'mountain' below. When the unit is completed, you will have a mountain full of information telling what you have learned about the Rockies. When your lists are finished, you may want to color the mountain.

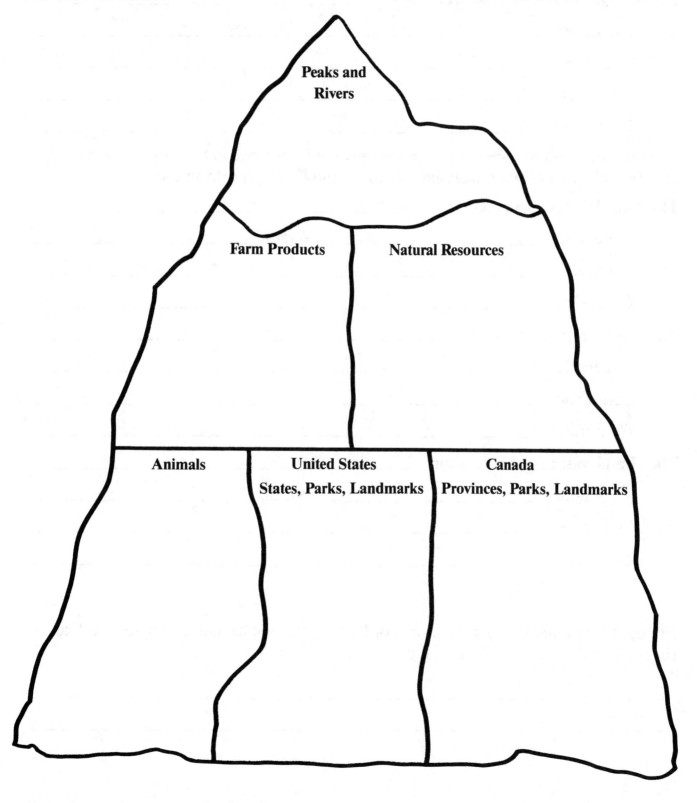

It's a Rocky World

More than 3,000 miles (4,800 kilometers) long and 350 miles (563 kilometers) wide, the Rocky Mountains are the largest mountain system in North America. Just where are the Rocky Mountains?

The Rocky Mountains: Highest elevation: _____

Continent: _____

Countries: _____

States: _____

Provinces: _____

The Rocky Mountains are not the only large mountain range in the world. Use a world map or globe to locate these mountain ranges and fill in the information:

The Alps: Highest elevation: _____

Length: _____ Width: _____

Continent: _____

Countries: _____

The Andes: Highest elevation: _____

Length: _____ Width: _____

Continent: _____

Countries: _____

The Himalayas: Highest elevation: _____

Length: _____ Width: _____

Continent: _____

Countries: _____

Put the four mountain ranges above in order with the one having the highest peak at the top and the one with the lowest peak at the bottom.

_____   _____

_____   _____

A Beastly Life

The Rocky Mountains are the home of a variety of animals, including mountain goats, bighorn sheep, elk, mink, mountain lions, coyotes, moose, and muskrats. Choose one of these animals. Read about it. Then pretend you are that animal. Write a paragraph telling what your life in the Rocky Mountains is like. You might describe where you live, what you eat, what you do, what the climate is like, who your enemies are, etc. Draw a picture of this animal above the paragraph.

My Life as a _____

_____

_____

_____

_____

_____

_____

_____

_____

_____

_____

_____

_____

_____

Rocky Mountain Recipes

Though it may be hard to imagine farming in the mountains, farmers in the Rockies raise both crops and livestock. Three of the more unusual products grown in the Rocky Mountains are chili peppers, pinto beans and sugar beets. Choose one of these Rocky Mountain food products and fill in the outline below:

Food: _____

I. Where is this product grown?

    A. _____

    B. _____

II. What climate is best for this product?

    A. _____

    B. _____

III. How is this product used?

    A. _____

    B. _____

What does this food look like
when it's harvested?
Draw a picture.

Have you ever tasted this food?
Describe the taste:

_____

_____

_____

My Rocky Mountain Recipe

Find a recipe using your food product. Write the recipe here.

Ingredients	Directions
_____	_____
_____	_____
_____	_____
_____	_____
_____	_____
_____	_____

Rocky Resources

Gold, lead, silver, tungsten, zinc, petroleum, natural gas, coal, uranium, copper and lumber are some of the Rocky Mountain region's major natural resources. Look up each resource. Find two uses for each one.

Gold 1. _____ 2. _____

Lead 1. _____ 2. _____

Silver 1. _____ 2. _____

Tungsten 1. _____ 2. _____

Zinc 1. _____ 2. _____

Petroleum 1. _____ 2. _____

Gas 1. _____ 2. _____

Coal 1. _____ 2. _____

Uranium 1. _____ 2. _____

Copper 1. _____ 2. _____

Lumber 1. _____ 2. _____

What are the natural resources in your state or province? Where are they found? How are they used?

Resource	Location	Use
_____	_____	_____
_____	_____	_____

Eureka!

Suppose you were a prospector looking for gold in the Rocky Mountains a hundred years ago.

Where would you look for gold? _____

_____

How would you mine for gold? _____

_____

How would you transport it? _____

_____

What are some of the dangers you would face? _____

_____

Eureka! You've struck it rich! And you've brought in your bags of gold to be weighed at the local mining office. Check the scales below. How much gold do you have in each bag?

☐ = 5 ounces/grams   △ = 10 ounces/grams

○ = 25 ounces/grams   ▭ = 50 ounces/grams

Rocky Recreation

There are national parks in both the American and Canadian Rockies. Two of the most famous are Glacier National Park and Yellowstone National Park. Draw something you might see if you went to each one.

Glacier National Park	**Yellowstone National Park**

The Rockies are also a good place for outdoor sports such as skiing, mountain climbing, white water rafting, hunting, fishing, camping and *spelunking* (cave exploring). Which Rocky Mountain sport would you like best? On the left, draw a picture of yourself participating in that sport. On the right, answer the questions relating to the sport.

Super _____
        (Sport)

Where would you go to do this?

_____

_____

What would you wear?

_____

_____

What equipment would you need?

_____

_____

What are the dangers of the sport?

_____

_____

What is the object (goal) of the sport?

_____

_____

What skills do you need to do well in this sport?

_____

_____

Easy Indian Crafts

Many Indian tribes, such as the Navajo, Shoshone, and Ute have lived in the Rocky Mountains. Read a book or story about one of these Indian tribes to see what you can learn about the way they live. Make an Indian headband, warrior's medal and beads!

Headband:

1. Cut a strip of paper about 3 inches wide and 8 inches long.

2. Cut a piece of yarn about 24 inches long.

3. Tape the yarn across the middle of the paper strip so an equal length of yarn hangs over each end of the paper.

4. Fold the top of the paper down and the bottom of the paper up, enclosing the yarn inside the paper.

5. Tape the paper together.

6. Decorate the band with Indian picture writing.

7. Use the yarn to tie the headband around your forehead.

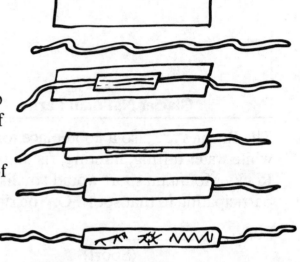

Warrior Medal:

1. Cut a circle of cardboard.

2. Cover the circle with glue.

3. Starting in the middle, glue down spirals of colored yarn, covering the whole circle. Add hanging yarn or bead decorations.

4. Braid together 3 long pieces of yarn to make the chain.

5. Tie the chain in a loop and attach medallion to the chain.

Beads:

Indian men and women wore beads of shells, animal claws, and even popcorn! Make a bead necklace from rolled paper beads, painted nut shells or thread spools, buttons, etc. Research this craft and make your own creative design.

People and Places © THE MONKEY SISTERS, INC.

Westward Ho!

Crossing the Rocky Mountains today is no problem. Modern highways go over and through the highest ridges. Trains connect the eastern and western coasts of Canada and the United States. Airplanes fly over the mountains. Early explorers and pioneers had a much harder time crossing the Rockies.

1. How did the pioneers travel across the mountains? _____

   _____

2. What were the hardships of such travel? _____

   _____

3. What were some of the dangers? _____

   _____

4. The pioneers couldn't take many belongings with them. Why? _____

5. Suppose you were making such a trip and were only allowed to take five of your

   belongings. What would you take? 1. _____

   2. _____ 3. _____ 4. _____

   5. _____

6. The pioneers often had to leave their belongings along the trail when the wagon was too heavy for their teams to pull up the steep mountain grades. They would throw away the least useful, heaviest things first. Look at your five belongings above. Suppose you had to throw them out, one at a time, to make it over the mountain. What would go first? Last?

   1. _____ 2. _____ 3. _____

   4. _____ 5. _____

Pretend you are a pioneer child keeping a diary of your wagon trip with your family across the mountains. Write about one day of your trip below. What did you see and do? How did you feel?

Dear Diary,

_____

_____

_____

_____

_____

_____

New York City

INTRODUCTION: View a travel film about the city and/or an educational film about its history. Share travel guides from your local automobile association or travel agencies. Brainstorm lists of what students know about New York City, what they would expect to see there, what the city is known for, etc. Students who have been to New York could share their memories and impressions with the class.

CURRICULUM AREA/SKILLS:	ACTIVITY/TITLE	PAGE NO.

Bulletin board   **"The Big Apple"**   No activity page

Divide a large bulletin board in half. On one side, put a large cutout of an apple and label it "The Big Apple." As the unit progresses, add student-contributed photos, words and symbols (thespian masks for theaters; swatches of cloth for the garment district, etc.) to show what New York is well-known for. Do the same for your school's city or town on the other half of the board.

Reading maps and schedules   **"Getting There"**   42

Obtain bus, train and flight schedules showing connections to New York City. Show routes on a map from your area to New York City. Students compare travel times and benefits of the various modes of transportation to get to New York.

Map reading; social studies   **"Map Math"**   43

Students count and identify bridges, bays, rivers, tunnels and boroughs and label them on an outline map provided. Provide detailed maps of New York City for students to work from. (The World Book, under New York, has an excellent N.Y.C. map.)

Language arts; writing   **"Sights to See"**   44

Using tourist guidebooks, students write two sentences about each of five major tourist attractions, describing the attraction and explaining its significance. They also research and list additional sights they would like to see.

Writing sentences; research   **"Over, Under, Across and Through"**   45

Students describe and illustrate three types of city superstructures: the suspension bridge, the subway and the skyscraper and explain how each has been important to New York City's growth.

Language arts; creative writing   **"Be an Author!"**   46

Discuss New York's position in the publishing industry. Look at books in your class or school library to see where they were published. Discuss the process of getting a book published and printed. Students then write and illustrate a book, write a short letter to an editor describing the book and a short review of a book authored by another student in class.

Art; careers   **"Fashions of the Future"**   47

Students find out about various careers in the fashion industry and design their own 'outfit' of the future. Look at fashion magazines and compare styles of various designers.

Writing; drama   **"On Broadway"**   48

Students write a short scene from New York City's early history—the capture of Captain Kidd or the purchase of Manhattan. Then they act out the scene for the class.

Language arts; research   **"Lots of Good Sports"**   49

Students research New York City's major sports teams, finding out league standings, symbols and colors, and star players for each team.

Social studies; art   **"Melting Pot, Meeting Spot"**   50

Read about the United Nations. Students research the origins and purpose of the United Nations and draw flags of some of the member nations. Discuss cultural heritage of your local area and ethnic heritage of the class. Have students ask parents if any of their relatives came to America through Ellis Island. Read the inscription on the Statue of Liberty.

CULMINATION: Have students read through recent magazines and newspapers and collect articles about current events in New York City. List current plays on Broadway, any annual events that may be taking place (Macy's Thanksgiving Day Parade, New York Marathon), people of New York 'in the news', etc. Place articles and any accompanying photos on a bulletin board and label "What's New in New York?"

       People and Places © THE MONKEY SISTERS, INC.

Getting There

How far are you from New York City? _____

How could you get there? List a few ways.

A. _____ B. _____ C. _____

     D. _____ E. _____

What does each mode of transportation offer? Let's find out!

Going by car:

Approximately how many miles or kilometers away is New York City? _____

How long would it take to get there? _____

What routes would you take if you went to New York by car? _____

What is a benefit of driving to New York? _____

Going by train:

How long would it take from where you live? _____

Where would you leave from to get a train to New York City? _____

What is a benefit of taking a train to New York? _____

Going by airplane:

How long would it take from where you live? _____

What airport would you leave from to fly to New York City? _____

Would you have to make a connecting flight? _____ Where? _____

What are two airports you could fly to in New York City? _____

What is a benefit of flying to New York? _____

Going by bus:

How long would it take from where you live? _____

Where would you leave from to get a bus to New York? _____

What is a benefit of taking a bus to New York? _____

Which way would *you* go? _____

Why? _____

_____

Map Math

Compare the outline map below to a detailed map of New York City.

1. How many boroughs are in New York City? _____
   Label each borough on the map below.

2. How many rivers run through New York City? _____
   Label each river.

3. Label these bridges and tunnels:
   - the Verrazano-Narrows Bridge
   - the Brooklyn Bridge
   - the Manhattan Bridge
   - the Williamsburg Bridge
   - the Triborough Bridge
   - the George Washington Bridge
   - the Bronx-Whitestone Bridge
   - the Holland Tunnel
   - the Lincoln Tunnel
   - the Brooklyn Battery Tunnel

Extra Credit! Research to find the answers to these questions:

1. How many miles does New York City extend east-west? _____

2. How many kilometers does New York City extend north-south? _____

3. How much of the Hudson River runs through New York City?

_____ miles _____ kilometers

People and Places © THE MONKEY SISTERS, INC.

Sights to See

It would probably take days, if not weeks, to see all of New York City's famous attractions. Using a tourist guidebook, write two sentences about each of the following popular sights. (1) Describe the attraction. (2) Tell why it is famous.

The Statue of Liberty

1. _____   2. _____

_____   _____

_____   _____

The Empire State Building

1. _____   2. _____

_____   _____

_____   _____

Radio City Music Hall

1. _____   2. _____

_____   _____

_____   _____

St. Patrick's Cathedral

1. _____   2. _____

_____   _____

_____   _____

Central Park

1. _____   2. _____

_____   _____

_____   _____

Name five other sights you would like to see if you visited New York City.

_____

_____

_____

Name _____

Over, Under, Across and Through

New York City has about 26,000 people per square mile. That's a lot of people in a small amount of space. Over the years, engineers and city planners and developed *superstructures* to allow them to build over, under, across and through New York City, connecting the five boroughs and making use of every available piece of land. Below are a few of the superstructures you will find in New York City. Explain what each structure is and how it has helped New York City grow. Name and illustrate one New York City example of each.

SKYSCRAPER	A skyscraper is a _____ NY needs skyscrapers because _____ The _____ is a NY skyscraper _____ and is _____ stories high.
BRIDGE	A suspension bridge is a _____ NY needs suspension bridges because _____ One famous NY bridge is the _____.
SUBWAY CAR	A subway is a _____ NY needs subways because _____ NYC's subway runs *under*ground. The part that runs *above* ground is called _____.

Be an Author!

New York City is the publishing capital of the United States. *Before* a book is published, the author writes to an editor of a publishing company to see if they are interested and want to read it. *After* the book is published, a book reviewer writes an article to tell people if they should read it.

1. Take four pieces of paper. Fold them in half. Staple along the fold. You now have a 16-page book.

2. Write a story in your book and illustrate it if you wish. Your book can be non-fiction (true) or fiction (fake).

Write a letter to an editor telling him or her about your book.

Dear Editor,

    I have just written a book called _____

_____

_____

_____

_____

_____

_____

Sincerely,

_____

Read a few of the books your classmates have written. Choose one of the books you liked best and write a *book review* telling other classmates why they should read it.

(Title)_____ by _____

_____ is a good book because _____

_____

_____

_____

_____

Reviewed by: _____

Look in the Sunday edition of a newspaper and bring in a book review.

Fashions of the Future

King of New York City's 300-plus manufacturing businesses is the *garment industry.*
What type of work would you do if you were a New York . . .

1. Designer: _____

2. Seamstress/Tailor: _____

3. Buyer: _____

4. Model: _____

5. Fashion Columnist: _____

Some of the world's most famous designers live in New York. An *original*—an outfit a
designer creates for one specific customer—can cost thousands of dollars. Design an
original of your own! Create an outfit for the 'model' below . . . something a boy or
girl your age might wear to a party in the year 2000. Give the model a hairstyle to go
with the outfit. Be creative and daring!

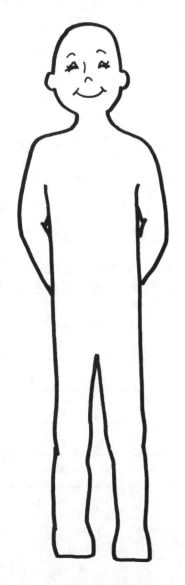
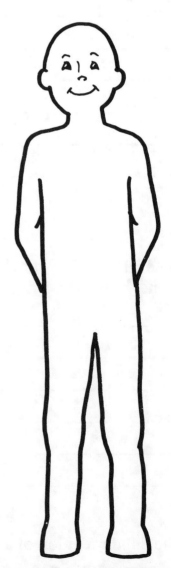

On Broadway

Broadway, the heart of New York City's theater district, is one of the most famous streets in the world. Every playwright dreams of having his or her play become a hit on Broadway and winning a Tony Award for the year's best play. Work with a partner and write a short, two-character play about one of the events in New York City's early history.

A. Dutch Governor Peter Minuit buys Manhattan island from an Indian chief for $24 in beads and cloth.

B. Captain Kidd, the famous pirate who lived on Wall Street, is captured by a British soldier to be tried and hanged in England.

_____ : _____
(character 1)   _____

_____ : _____
(character 2)   _____

_____ : _____
(character 1)   _____

_____ : _____
(character 2)   _____

_____ : _____
(character 1)   _____

_____ : _____
(character 2)   _____

_____ : _____
(character 1)   _____

_____ : _____
(character 2)   _____

Act out your play for the class. Who will win the class Tony Award?

Name _____

Lots of Good Sports

New York City is the home of several major sports teams. See what you can find out about these teams.

Team Name	Sport	League	Record—Last Season	Colors & Symbols	Star Players
YANKEES					
GIANTS					
METS					
RANGERS					
JETS					
KNICKS					
ISLANDERS					

People and Places © THE MONKEY SISTERS, INC.

Melting Pot, Meeting Spot

New York City was once called a "melting pot" because people of all nations came to New York, became U.S. citizens, and blended their cultures together to make up modern America. The Statue of Liberty greeted these *immigrants* from all over the world, a symbol of welcome, peace and freedom. Today New York City is still a meeting place for people from all over the world. More than 150 countries meet at the United Nations, a newer symbol of world peace. Can you answer these questions about the United Nations?

1. When was the United Nations founded? _____

2. How many countries were members when the United Nations began? _____

3. Where is the United Nations building in New York City? _____

4. What is the purpose or goal of the United Nations? _____

5. What do these United Nations organizations do?

   UNICEF _____

   World Health Organization _____

6. Who is your country's representative to the United Nations at this time? _____

Outside the United Nations building in New York City are flags from all the member nations. Use an encyclopedia to find out what the flags of these countries look like. Draw these flags.

Japan	Canada	Great Britain	Ireland
USSR (Russia)	China	France	Israel

Where did your ancestors come from? _____

The Great Lakes

INTRODUCTION: View a film about the Great Lakes region. Discuss the difference between fresh water and salt water, lakes and oceans, lakes and rivers.

CULMINATION; (1) Plan a Great Lakes vacation! Get travel brochures for various cities, parks and historical sites in the area. Individually, or in small groups, plan a week's outing in the Great Lakes region. Where would students go? What would they want to see and do? (2) Read or listen to segments of Longfellow's *Hiawatha,* the story of an Indian brave who lived on the shores of the Great Lakes.

A Great Lake!

Draw an outline map of one of the Great Lakes. Draw in any major islands. Mark all the states or provinces which border the lake. Show the locations of five major towns or cities on the lakefront and any canals and rivers that join the lake. Color the map.

Lake _____

The Great Lake Monster

Have you ever heard of *Nessie, the Loch Ness Monster*? This dinosaur-like creature is said to live beneath the waters of Loch Ness, a lake in Scotland. Some people even claim to have taken her photograph!

Suppose a monster lived in the waters of Lake Superior, the largest and deepest of the Great Lakes. On the right below, write a poem or short story about the day you went fishing on Lake Superior and caught *Gressie, the Great Lakes Monster.* What was she like? What did you do with her? How did she feel about being caught in your net? On the left below, draw the 'photograph' you took of Gressie.

A Monstrous Catch

_____

_____

_____

_____

_____

_____

_____

_____

_____

_____

_____

_____

_____

_____

_____

People and Places © THE MONKEY SISTERS, INC.

Bulldozers Made of Ice

What does a bulldozer do? _____

_____

_____

A *glacier,* a gigantic, moving block of ice, works much like a natural bulldozer, digging out dirt, pushing aside rocks and trees in its path. The Great Lakes were formed millions of years ago by these natural bulldozers. See if you can figure out how it was done by putting the steps below in the correct order. Put a **1** next to the sentence that tells what happened first, a **2** next to what happened second, and so on. Number **6** will be the last.

_____ A. The glacier picked up the rocks and dirt from the holes and pushed them forward.

_____ B. As the climate got colder, glaciers—huge mountains of ice—began moving South.

_____ C. The weight and force of the glaciers started digging out huge holes in the earth.

_____ D. The holes the glacier had dug began to fill up with the melting ice water.

_____ E. The mounds of dirt and rock held the water in, forming the Great Lakes.

_____ F. As the climate got warmer, the glaciers began to melt and move northward again.

Illustrate any one of the steps above. Draw a picture to show one way a glacier 'bulldozer' formed the Great Lakes.

Which step did you illustrate? _____

If you wanted to see a glacier today, where would you go?

_____

Borders in Order

The Great Lakes form part of the border between two countries. What are they?

_____ and _____

Going from East to West, what states lie on the border between the United States and Canada?

_____

_____

What forms the four borders (north, south, east, west) of each of the five Great Lakes?

Lake	North	South	East	West
Lake Superior				
Lake Michigan				
Lakes Huron				
Lake Erie				
Lake Ontario				

What forms the four borders of each of the following?

Place	North	South	East	West
Your country				
Your state or province				
Your school				
Your house or apartment building				

People and Places © THE MONKEY SISTERS, INC.

Cities on the Lake

Cities have been built on both the American and Canadian shores of the Great Lakes. Why were the lakeshores good locations to build cities and towns?

1. _____

2. _____

3. _____

4. _____

List four American and four Canadian cities on the shores of the Great Lakes.

American Cities	**Canadian Cities**
1. _____	1. _____
2. _____	2. _____
3. _____	3. _____
4. _____	4. _____

Choose one American and one Canadian city. See if you can find the answers to the following questions about each one.

American City: _____   Canadian City: _____

On Lake: _____   On Lake: _____

Year founded: _____   Year founded: _____

Population: _____   Population: _____

Major industries: _____   Major industries: _____

_____   _____

_____   _____

Important events in history: Important events in history:

_____   _____

_____   _____

Landmarks to see: Landmarks to see:

_____   _____

_____   _____

Water Ways

A *canal* is a ditch that carries water from one place to another. Some canals are small, like irrigation ditches used in farming. Others are big enough to carry the largest cargo ships. Three of the most famous canals ever built are the Erie Canal, the Suez Canal and the Panama Canal. The first paragraph below gives some information about the Erie Canal. Use an encyclopedia to get the information you will need to fill in the second paragraph about either the Suez Canal or the Panama Canal.

The Erie Canal

The Erie Canal opened in 1825. With a total of 82 locks, the 363-mile (584-kilometer) long canal went from Albany to Buffalo, New York and connected the waters of Lake Erie to the waters of the Hudson River. Before the Canal was built, people had to travel by horse or wagon. The canal was dug out by men using shovels and other hand tools. The first boats to use the canal were canal boats pulled by horses on tow-paths along the shore.

The _____ Canal

The _____ Canal opened in _____.

With a total of _____ locks, the _____-mile long canal went

from _____ to _____

and connected the waters of _____ with the waters

of _____. Before the canal was built,

people had to travel _____.

The canal was dug out by _____

_____. The first boats to use the canal

were _____.

_____

●●●

Fierce winds, known as Northwesters, are common on the Great Lakes. Sudden storms were a real danger to early ships. The popular American folk song, *The Wreck of the Edmund Fitzgerald,* tells the story of one ship that sank during such a storm on the Great Lakes—with 29 men aboard.

Suppose you were the radio operator on a ship in danger of sinking in a storm. Your radio is out, but you can still send a message in *Morse Code,* a system of dots (short sounds) and dashes (longer sounds) that stand for different letters of the alphabet. For example, ●●●　　●●　　●●● means **S.O.S.** or **Save Our Ship**, a call for help recognized almost everywhere.

Here is the code. It's up to you to send a message. What kind of ship are you on? How many people on the crew? What are you hauling? What condition is the ship in? What kind of help do you need? Where are you? Whom will you call? Write your message—in Morse Code—below.

A	●—	**M**	——	**X**	●—●●
B	—●●●	**N**	—●	**Y**	●● ●●
C	●● ●	**O**	●●	**Z**	●●● ●
D	—●●	**P**	●●●●●	**1**	●——●
E	●	**Q**	●—●	**2**	●●—●●
F	●—●	**R**	● ●●	**3**	●●●—●
G	——●	**S**	●●●	**4**	●●●●—
H	●●●●	**T**	—	**5**	———
I	●●	**U**	●●—	**6**	●●●●●● ●
J	—●—●	**U**	●●● ●	**7**	——●●
K	—●—	**V**	●●●—	**8**	—●●●●
L	—	**W**	●——	**9**	—●●—
				0	—

This code was used in the U.S. and Canada. Operators in other countries used a slightly different international code.

People and Places © THE MONKEY SISTERS, INC. 58.

Lake on a String

The Great Lakes are major shipping centers. What kinds of boats and ships could you see *on* one of the Great Lakes?

A. _____   B. _____

C. _____   D. _____

The Great Lakes are major industrial, commercial and recreation areas. What might you see *around* the shores of one of the Great Lakes?

A. _____   B. _____

C. _____   D. _____

The Great Lakes form the largest body of fresh water on Earth. Although water pollution has been a problem, many kinds of marine life make their home *in* the Great Lakes. What might you see if you went diving in the Great Lakes?

A. _____   B. _____

C. _____   D. _____

Make a Lake Mobile

1. Get a wire hanger.

2. Draw the following on cardboard or stiff paper:
   A. One ship you might see *on* the lake.
   B. Two things you might see *around* the lakeshore.
   C. The lake itself.
   D. Two things you might see *in* the lake.

3. Cut out the items you have drawn.

4. Use string to attach the items to the hanger as shown in the illustration.

5. Hang your 'lake mobile' in your classroom or in your room at home.

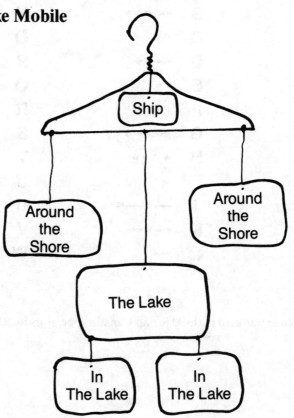

59.

Following Orders

When we tell a story, we usually tell it in *chronological order.* That means we tell it in the order it happened.

When you describe a group of things, you have many orders to choose from:

1. *Random order* really means no particular order at all.

   List the five Great Lakes in *random order.*

   _____ _____ _____ _____ _____

   List the names of five classmates in *random order.*

   _____ _____ _____ _____ _____

2. *Order of size* can be biggest to smallest, or smallest to biggest. (Height, weight, area, population, etc.)

   List the five Great Lakes in *order of size* from smallest to largest.

   _____ _____ _____ _____ _____

   List the five classmates from above *in order of size* from shortest to tallest.

   _____ _____ _____ _____ _____

3. *Spatial order* means the order in which things occupy space. For example, you could describe the things in your classroom from front to back, left to right, clockwise, etc.

   List the five Great Lakes in *spatial order* from west to east.

   _____ _____ _____ _____ _____

   List the five students above in *spatial order* according to where they sit in the classroom from left to right or front to back.

   _____ _____ _____ _____ _____

4. Here are some other orders to follow.

   A. List five members of your family *in order of age* from youngest to oldest.

      _____ _____ _____ _____ _____

   B. List five political offices in your country *in order of rank* from highest to lowest.

      _____ _____ _____ _____ _____

   C. List five of your favorite belongings *in order of importance* with the most important to you first.

      _____ _____ _____ _____ _____